LIFE BEGINS AT 70

THE DAWN OF A NEW ERA

ALFRED BELLANTI

LIFE BEGINS AT 70

THE DAWN OF A NEW ERA

ALFRED BELLANTI

Disclaimer

Every care has been taken to ensure that the knowledge in this book is accurate. Medical procedures referred to in this book have come from scientific papers. Self-administration of medical techniques is not advised. Consultation with your doctor is recommended if you want to use any of the techniques because of the dangers of side effects. Your doctor could formulate treatment specific to you. Success using the knowledge and techniques provided in this book may vary from person to person depending on how well the knowledge is applied and how thoroughly it is applied. The book is very helpful but is not intended as a total substitute for consultation with your doctor.

First Printing: May 2023
Hardcover ISBN 978-0-6489582-5-3
Paperback ISBN 978-0-6489582-6-0

Book Interior and E-Book Design by Amit Dey

ENDORSEMENTS

"It's all about perspective! Alfred Bellanti has written an outstanding, inspirational book that challenges the popular media view that we are all 'over the hill' at 60!

I found this book to be truly life changing for me; it is well written and enjoyable to read, immediately challenged me to adopt a different mindset and then showed me how to do it!

I shall be providing it to my more mature clients without doubt! And actually many of my younger adult clients would benefit from the advice within its pages!"

—Jill Lien -
BIG HORN WELLNESS
Holistic Effective Transforming

"From the moment I saw the title of Alfred Bellanti's new book, Life Begins at 70, I knew that this is a must read book. We're all getting older, but how we age is a lot about attitude.

Turning 70 for me was the dawn of a new era. It's new-found freedom and the opportunity to make the most of each moment. I now have the liberty to ride my bike long distances, backpack in the mountains and explore this world.

Life Begins at 70 will show you how you can change your attitude, improve and maintain your health and vitality and offer you anti-aging tips."

—Roger Moore
Institute of Hypnotherapy

"The author is right on the ball. Antioxidants and amino acids are the key to everything. All the specifics are listed in the book."

—Anne Newman
- Retired Naturopathic Nutritionist,
Dip Nutrition, Rem Massage, Reiki, Bach Flowers

CHAPTERS

WHY I AM WRITING THIS BOOK

The intention behind writing this book is to give you, the reader, information that will excite you, motivate you, and serve as an example of how to tackle life once you reach that seventieth decade or before.

At the time of writing I looked for statistics about life expectancy. These are what I found

The current life expectancy for Australia in 2023 is 83.94 years.
The current life expectancy for the U.K. in 2023 is 81.77 years.
The current life expectancy for the U.S. in 2023 is 79.11 years.

I believe these figures are based on averages and have incorporated the many deaths that occurred with covid. Nevertheless people can live happy and healthy lives beyond the ages shown above. You will understand how when you read this book.

An early Danish Twin Study involving 2,872 Danish twin pairs had established that only about 20% of how long the average person lives is dictated by our genes, whereas the other 80% is dictated by our lifestyle. I have since found that about 60% of the 80% is within the individual's control.

I believe that self talk and attitude together with biological, environmental and other factors can influence aging. These factors will be discussed later in the book.

Though it is inevitable that we get old, have you ever noticed the difference between some older people of the same age? Why is it that some seem to drag themselves around while others stride around in a lively, youthful manner?

Do you think attitude has something to do with this? I remember back in my early twenties I was working in the accounts department of a film company. I had just begun a course at an evening college. Enthusiastic about this I told one of my work colleagues, barely ten years older than me. He replied "I would do a course too, but I'm too old now." Does that indicate a certain attitude on his part?

Furthermore I have noticed that certain individuals are kept alive and active by their job or profession. Once they are retired, or made redundant they seem to deteriorate and age rapidly. Why is that so?

I am now well into my seventies and still very active. I go for long walks, travel, paddle my kayak, play with a band, teach meditation and volunteer at a mental health recreation facility.

I read that the maximum survival potential of the human species was estimated to be 110 to 115 years (Matteson 1997.) Though I didn't agree with these figures at first, more research has brought out some interesting facts.

The sad reality is that only a small minority of the overall population survive past the age of 100 years. When this happens, it becomes newsworthy.

Nevertheless there are exceptions! Years ago I remember seeing a documentary about people living somewhere in the Georgian mountains where longevity was the norm. These people lived on subsistence farming. They worked in fields all day and came together in the evening for a meal of fresh produce and home made wine. Similar findings were made about the Japanese island Okinawa, where people had a diet consisting mainly of fish and vegetables. More will be said about nutrition in later chapters.

THE BLUE ZONES

Some of my colleagues already knew about "Blue Zones" but I had never heard of them until I was referred to an article from the American Journal of Lifestyle Medicine by a fellow writer. I acknowledge the author Dan Buettner and the editors of this article -

"What began as a National Geographic expedition discovered five places around the world where people consistently live over 100 years old. These areas were dubbed the Blue Zones and are widely spread around the globe. They are -

- Loma Linda, California USA
- Nicoya, Costa Rica
- Sardinia, Italy
- Ikaria, Greece
- Okinawa, Japan"

How these statistics have altered because of recent pandemics have still to be determined.

The aging process has been documented using several parameters, the main emphasis being on functionality. The functional ability of people is crucial to how they cope with activities of daily living which in turn affects their quality of life.

Functional status can be defined as a person's ability to perform the activities essential to ensure wellbeing. Biological, psychological and social factors are taken into account when assessing the overall functional status.

Biological factors are important. If the person has suffered a serious illness or injury this could take its toll on the body and hasten the aging process; or does it? How is it that some people, equal to each other in every way, can suffer the same illness or injury yet a number of them recover to live a vital and youthful life while the rest give up on life, age rapidly and die? Do you think psychological factors come into play here?

Connection with like minded people is important. I remember at one stage of my life having made fun of older ladies playing bingo at a local social club. That is until my mother started to do this. I nostalgically recall how lively she was on bingo days. Mum had made friends at the club. She enjoyed their company and many of her friends turned up to celebrate her ninetieth birthday.

Therefore social factors can be very important in maintaining a youthful outlook. Having the desire and energy to enjoy others' company versus being home alone and feeling miserable is something to consider.

Researchers involved in Blue Zones studies found that the lifestyles of all Blue Zones residents shared nine specific characteristics. These are called the Power 9.

"At first it seems that to make it to age 100, a person must have to win the genetic lottery. However, many individuals have the capacity to make it well into the early 90s and largely without chronic disease. The Blue Zones research uncovered 9 evidence-based common denominators among the world's centenarians that are believed to slow this aging process.

1. ***Move naturally***. The world's longest-lived people do not pump iron, run marathons, or join gyms. Instead, they live in environments that constantly nudge them into moving without thinking about it. They grow gardens and do not have mechanical conveniences for house and yard work.
2. ***Purpose***. The Okinawans call it *Ikigai* and the Nicoyans call it *plan de vida*; for both, it translates to "why I wake up in the morning." Knowing your sense of purpose is worth up to 7 years of extra life expectancy.
3. ***Downshift***. Even people in the Blue Zones experience stress. Stress leads to chronic inflammation, associated with every major age-related disease.

What the world's longest-lived people have that others do not are routines to shed that stress. Okinawans take a few moments each day to remember their ancestors; Adventists pray; Ikarians take a nap; and Sardinians do happy hour.

4. ***80% Rule. Hara hachi bu***—the Okinawan 2500-year old Confucian mantra said before meals reminds them to stop eating when their stomachs are 80% full. The 20% gap between not being hungry and feeling full could be the difference between losing weight or gaining it. People in the Blue Zones eat their smallest meal in the late afternoon or early evening, and then, they do not eat any more the rest of the night.
5. ***Plant slant.*** Beans, including fava, black, soy, and lentils, are the cornerstone of most centenarian diets. Meat—mostly pork—is eaten on average only 5 times per month. Serving sizes are 3 to 4 oz (85 to 113 grams), about the size of a deck of cards.
6. ***Wine at five.*** People in all Blue Zones (except Adventists) drink alcohol moderately and regularly. Moderate drinkers outlive nondrinkers. The trick is to drink 1 to 2 glasses per day (preferably Sardinian Cannonau wine), with friends and/or with food. And no, you cannot save up all week and have 14 drinks on Saturday.

7. ***Belong.*** All but 5 of the 263 centenarians interviewed belonged to some faith-based community. Denomination does not seem to matter. Research shows that attending faith-based services 4 times per month will add 4 to 14 years of life expectancy.
8. ***Loved ones first.*** Successful centenarians in the Blue Zones put their families first. This means keeping aging parents and grandparents nearby or in the home (it lowers disease and mortality rates of children in the home too.). They commit to a life partner (which can add up to 3 years of life expectancy) and invest in their children with time and love. (They'll be more likely to care for aging parents when the time comes.)
9. ***Right tribe.*** The world's longest lived people chose—or were born into—social circles that supported healthy behaviors, Okinawans created *moais*—groups of 5 friends that committed to each other for life. Research from the Framingham Studies shows that smoking, obesity, happiness, and even loneliness are contagious. So the social networks of long-lived people have favorably shaped their health behaviors."

Here are a few examples of some of the people from the Blue Zones locations who were interviewed. The full stories can be found here - Blue Zones - PMC

Loma Linda, California USA an Adventist community - Dr Ellsworth Wareham, 95 years old at the time, was told that a contractor wanted $6000 to build a privacy fence in his yard. Instead of paying the contractor he decided to do it himself. He finished the job in three days then went to hospital to perform open heart surgery, one of the twenty surgeries he performed per month.

Then there is Marge Jetton age 105, who woke up every morning at 5:30 am read her Bible, had a breakfast of slow cooked oatmeal, nuts, and dates with soy milk and a prune juice shot. She would then ride her stationary bike for thirty minutes and get in her Cadillac and drive to her volunteer jobs for seven different organizations.

Nicoya, Costa Rica - Nicoyans spend just 15% of what America does on health care and are more than twice as likely than Americans to reach a healthy age of 90 years. Faith and family play a strong role in Nicoyan culture. So does *plan de vida*, or reason to live, which helps Nicoyan elders maintain a positive outlook and active lifestyle. Nicoyans eat little to no processed foods but plenty of antioxidant-rich tropical fruit. But they also have 1 unique secret: calcium and magnesium-rich water, which wards off heart disease and promotes strong bones.

Sardinia, Italy - The cardio-vascular systems of this community of shepherds are strong because they graze their flocks over rugged mountainous territory that necessitates them to walk about five miles every day. The classic Sardinian diet is plant based, consisting of whole-grain bread, beans, garden vegetables, and fruits. They eat meat only on Sundays and special occasions and drink Cannonau wine moderately.

Ikaria, Greece - An Ikarian, Stamatis Moraitis, moved to America when he was 22 years old to pursue the American dream. He was a painter, and immediately started having success, bought a house, married, and had 3 kids. At the age of 66 years, he developed terminal lung cancer. Instead of dying in America, he decided to move back to Ikaria and moved in with his parents. He started breathing the air, drinking the wine, and eating a Mediterranean diet. After a few months, he planted a garden not planning on ever getting to harvest the vegetables; 37 years later he has a vineyard producing 200 L of wine a year. His secret he says? "I just forgot to die."

Okinawa, Japan - In Okinawa, at age 5, children are put into committed social networks called *moais*. In one of these the average age was 102 years.The Okinawa tradition of forming a *moai* provides secure social networks. These networks provide financial and emotional support in times of need and give their members the stress-shedding security of knowing there is always someone there for them. Okinawans also attribute their longevity to the old Confucian mantra said before meals *Hara Hachi Bu*, which reminds them to stop eating when 80% full, so they do not overeat. They also hold a strong sense of purpose in their family. One centenarian described the feeling of holding her great great great grandchild as "jumping into heaven."

RATE YOUR LEVEL OF YOUTHFULNESS

This table was modified from the quiz on liveup.org.au. You can use it to assess your level of youthfulness. Stay positive! No matter how you score there will be something or some way that will help you.

MOTIVATION How Interested Are You?	**Not at all**	**Slightly**	**Moder-ately**	**Very**	**Extremely**
Staying fit and healthy					
Connecting and spending time with like-minded people					
Hobbies, trying new things, Learning new skills					

ACTIVITIES	Not at all	Slightly	Moder-ately	Very	Extremely
How quickly can you walk up a decent hill					
How easily can you sit and get up from the floor					
How easily can you cut your toenails					

Now that you have filled the table you are more aware of where you are as far as youthfulness goes and you can take steps to get yourself up to scratch. If you find you are too deficient ask for help, use mobility aids, stay in the race and read on. There will be something in this book that will get you back on the path.

https://liveup.org.au/get-started

In USA there is an equivalent website that supports healthy aging and independent living -

https://www.agingresearch.org/

For UK readers, useful information could be found here -

https://www.gov.uk/government/publications/healthy-ageing/healthy-ageing-applying-all-our-health

WHAT CAUSES AGING

Before you read what science has discovered about the aging process, be assured that in most cases the process can at least be halted by changes in lifestyle and diet. It is also possible that physical rejuvenation can occur with these changes.

Science tells us that aging takes place because of shortening of our telomeres. Telomeres are the specific DNA-protein structures found at both ends of our chromosomes. They consist of the same short DNA sequence repeated over and over again.

For the sake of simplicity let's say that telomeres protect chromosomes from breaking down or going through unwanted changes. Each time cell division occurs a small portion of telomere is lost. The key to a longer, healthy life is to prevent or at least slow down the loss of telomeric DNA.

WHAT CAUSES LOSS OF TELOMERIC DNA -

Smoking - Many studies have been done on smokers to prove this.

Obesity - Studies on obese mice and humans propose that loss of telomeric DNA happens due to oxidative stress.

Toxic Work Environments - This was shown when contrasting office workers and traffic police officers who were exposed to traffic pollution.

Type of Work - Similarly analysis of lymphocytes from coke-oven workers showed evidence of telomere shortening. So too with shift workers.

Stress - High stress has shown to release glucocorticoid hormones which can through antioxidant reducing pathway shorten telomeres.

Polyunsaturated Fatty Acids - Greater intake of these, especially linoleic acid, and low intake of fiber was negatively associated with waist circumference and dietary intake of polyunsaturated fatty acids, especially linoleic acid.

Excessive Protein - The highest life expectancy of Japanese is associated with low protein and high-carbohydrate intake in diet.

WHAT SLOWS THE BREAKDOWN OF TELOMERIC DNA?

Omega 3 Fatty Acids - A diet containing antioxidant omega-3 fatty acids, which are antioxidants, are associated with reduced rate of telomere shortening. Moreover the consumption of a diet rich in antioxidants such as vitamin E, vitamin C, and beta-carotene was associated with longer telomeres and lower risk of breast cancer.

OTHER CONSIDERATIONS

Have you ever heard someone saying "age is just a number?" If so, what do you think of that?

I remember being told that when I was in my early seventies. I was on an excursion in the Grand Canyon with a group of people all of whom were younger than me.

We had walked a long way down a steep grade then it was time to walk back up. I remarked about my age to a young British girl who was a recently graduated teacher. She was the one who replied "age is just a number."

She then went on to say that people's age doesn't matter to her and the important thing was that I was there among the group doing the same thing as the others were doing.

Is it possible that reducing the level of activity as the years go by can contribute to more rapid aging? What do you think?

And this leads to another question. Is it possible that the way you think about yourself can influence the aging process? What I'm getting at here is that you need the right mindset. Think old and you create old; think young and you are more likely to retain a youthful outlook and slow down the aging process.

Then there are the obvious things that will cause aging. You've probably heard these before but must be included here as a matter of thoroughness -

Smoking - Anything at all - tobacco, marijuana, crack, ice, even vaping

Alcohol - Especially hard liquor and anything in excess

Junk food - Except maybe the occasional junk meal when traveling or away from home

Overeating - Overeating on a regular basis puts more stress on the body than eating moderately

Stress - Excessive continual stress can have its toll on the body though we all need a certain amount of stress to maintain homeostasis.

MY STORY

Telling you about myself comes from a gut feeling that what I tell you will be helpful to you. While writing this I am asking myself whether this is coming from the ego, and if it is, then so be it. I believe an altruistic motive is mixed in with this so-called "ego" and I am here to help you, not just to brag. So I shall begin with a brief autobiography -

I was born under British Rule in the far off land of Egypt.

"How was that?" You may ask.

Well, back in those days the British Empire stretched far and wide. Mum and Dad were born in Egypt from mixed heritage and were designated as "British Subjects." Hence I was born a "British Subject" too.

The 1940s was the era of "Swing," a musical genre that was to influence me later in my life. If you want to follow up on examples of this music, find "Tuxedo Junction", "In the Mood", "Boogie Woogie Bugle Boy" on Youtube.

During World War II Dad served in the RAF (Royal Air Force) as an anti-aircraft gunner stationed in Heliopolis, near Cairo. The posting had been established because of an anticipated invasion by the Nazi Luftwaffe. Rommel's tank squadron had already been operating in nearby Sahara.

Mum gave birth to me in the RAF Base Hospital, Heliopolis just after the end of the war. Therefore I was conceived as a war baby. Watch out!

Mum and Dad then moved back to Port Said where they had been living before the war. Port Said for those who are not familiar with the African Continent is at the Mediterranean entrance to the Suez Canal.The Suez Canal was excavated in the nineteenth century following a plan by a French engineer Ferdinand De Lesseps. Because of this there was also a heavy French influence in Egypt and an Italian influence that dated back to Roman times as a result of the liaison between Anthony and Cleopatra.

My education as a child was firstly with Italian nuns, then French brothers and before leaving Egypt, a year at a privately run English School. My gratitude extends to the fact that I can speak three languages. English has now become my primary language. I am the eldest of two sisters and a brother.

For those of you who do not know the history, the Egyptian people became discontent that revenue from the Suez Canal was flowing out of Egypt. The Suez Canal Company was run by foreigners who employed foreign tugboat

Port Said Egypt - Mediterranean Ocean in the background

pilots to navigate freighters and passenger liners through tricky spots along the canal.

Hence the foreigners were ousted from Egypt in 1956 but the British, not accepting this, came back by force. Shelling Port Said from the Mediterranean, then landing troops who killed many Egyptian soldiers and civilians who put up resistance.

My family was still in Port Said at the time. The passenger liner "Orion" for which Dad had booked passage to Australia could not dock at Port Said and we were stranded until the fighting stopped after which we were evacuated to Italy by an Italian Red Cross vessel.

We spent a few weeks with some relatives in the countryside until dad, by selling a few remaining assets, was able to buy passage on a liner to Australia. The Suez Canal was still blocked at the time so the liner had to travel down the west coast of Africa making two stops. One at Dakar, the other at Cape Town, which then pointed us toward the west coast of Australia, still a long way away. Had the Suez Canal still been opened, the total journey would have been shortened by at least half.

The ship stopped at Fremantle. I remember going ashore with the family and catching a bus to Perth. We would have settled in Perth except that Mum's parents and other relatives were established in the suburbs of Sydney. They had migrated a few years earlier when the political situation in Egypt began to be unstable. King Farouk, the reigning monarch had been overthrown and exiled to Italy and a strong feeling of nationalism had begun to rise.

We were warmly met by relatives at the wharf and driven to the house in the suburbs where we stayed for a number of months until with the combined efforts of Grandpa and my Dad a house was purchased. Until then the six of us Mum, Dad, brother and two sisters shared the same room together. Double bed bunks made this possible.

School was a difficult adjustment because though I had learned the English language, the Australian vernacular and pronunciation was hard to understand. I was a bright pupil and was encouraged to sit for a bursary that would have paid for my secondary education. In those days dictation was one of the skills taught. The teacher would read a passage from a book, and we had to write down the correctly spelled words as they were being dictated.

Though I was never told, I believe I missed out on the bursary because I either misunderstood the pronunciation and wrote the wrong word or wrote the correct word as was heard by the pronunciation. Nevertheless I went ahead to junior high school where I scored well in all examinations with credits in the main subjects. Unknown to me the school was going to close and no new enrolments were being taken.

My brother, who was coming out from kindergarten, had to begin primary classes at a different school and Mum wanted me to transfer to that school so that I could look after my brother.

That was when things changed for me. It turned out this other school was at a much higher standard than the previous one. The calculus and analytical geometry being taught went right over my head, partly because of how fast it was presented, and also because I was tired, trying to keep up with school, homework, and an evening newspaper delivery job. To cut a long story short, I did very badly at the end of the year and decided I wouldn't go back. I went to work as a clerk for a few years.

I caught up with the high school subjects at an evening college and gained admission into university. This led to a bachelor degree and other diplomas. In 1993 I started my practice as a Clinical Hypnotherapist. In 1999 I added Botanical Medicine to my practice. That led to getting a part time job in the vitamins department of a large pharmacy.

In 2002 I was struck down with anaplastic large cell lymphoma (a cancer) near the pancreas. A laparotomy and biopsy were performed to confirm this diagnosis. Chemotherapy followed. The laparotomy led to recurring ascites that required additional hospitalization. My gut has hardly ever fully recovered since.

Nevertheless after about eighteen months of recovery time I took on a job in a call center where I could sit at a phone in front of a computer screen and respond to customer enquiries via telephone and email. Continuing to see hypnotherapy clients on evenings and weekends.

During that time I received a telephone call from Angela, a former supervisor of the pharmacy where I had worked prior to the cancer. Angela was now the supervisor at another pharmacy. This pharmacy prepared and sold herbal and homeopathic remedies as well as pharmaceuticals. Angela asked if I would like to fill in for a colleague who was on extended leave. I gladly filled the position.

Years later, my energy level unexpectedly dropped and I became immobile. The ascites returned! A cardiologist discovered that my cardiac muscle had been damaged by one of the ingredients of the chemotherapy I had received fourteen years previously. The cardiologist confirmed a diagnosis of congestive heart failure. I was prescribed three different medications to be taken daily for this. I am still using these meds at the time of writing.

Currently I do daily walks, brief repetitions with two 5 Kg (11 lbs) dumbbells and the occasional kayaking when weather and tides are favorable.

I also meditate twice daily, facilitate a meditation session once a week and volunteer at a mental health recreational center. Recently I applied to volunteer as a health educator in a local government run center for seniors. Then there is the sporadic overseas travel which is always invigorating, even though it seems tiring at the time.

ABOUT PREVENTION OF EARLY AGING

The following information is from a Scientific American article By Jennifer C. Lovejoy - Using Data to Live Longer, Healthier Lives:

"More than a decade ago, a group of us at the Institute for Systems Biology in Seattle began to think about how the practice of medicine could focus more on wellness than disease. Rather than waiting until people get sick, what if we found ways of helping people stay healthy?

Part of what inspired this question was the tremendous amount of data becoming available through advances in technology, such as low-cost genetic sequencing. These tools emerged from "multiomics", which collectively refers to new data-driven fields of inquiry into the body's many biological constituents. The "omics" in the name comes from the common methods used to analyze four different types of constituents: proteins (proteomics), metabolites (metabolomics), genes (genomics) and gut bacteria (microbiomics).

Since then, we've developed these ideas and honed them through research with thousands of people. We've found that the copious "omic" data becoming available gives clinicians an opportunity not only to diagnose disease, but also to take the measure of an individual's state of wellness. We are developing ways of using this data to identify early signs that things are going off track—in other words, when a person begins the transition from wellness to illness. And we are fashioning interventions that get them back on track before and during this disease transition, sometimes avoiding disease entirely.

These interventions need not be drastic or invasive. Even small changes to diet and exercise or targeted supplements could potentially head off obesity, diabetes, heart disease and other ailments before they have a chance to develop. The key is to intervene early, before the onset of disease. By combining these interventions with behavioral science, we've been able to deliver interventions that people actively incorporate into their daily lives, often with dramatic results.

We are now focused on filling the research gaps in our understanding of disease transitions and how to prevent them—what we have come to call "scientific wellness." At the same time, we need to remove many practical roadblocks to realize a truly preventive and personalized approach to medicine. But nevertheless, our work has demonstrated unequivocally that this approach could vastly improve health-care outcomes compared with today's disease-centric medicine. And because it is preventive, it could generate considerable cost savings."

Lovejoy goes on to inform the readers about THE PIONEER 100 PROJECT.

"For this pilot study 108 healthy volunteers were recruited to participate in a nine-month study seeking to both quantify and optimize wellness. Baseline data was gathered which later would be used to develop action plans, perform scientific research and assess the program's success.

The data was collected on a variety of health measures. Rather than rely on surveys of food intake, which are notoriously unreliable, it measured nutritional biomarkers - molecules in the blood that give a more accurate indication of what an individual is eating.

In general, this study relied on measurements of biomarkers, which could be made with precision, rather than self-reported disease or conditions.

The volunteers wore Fitbits that monitored their physical activity and sleep. A variety of lifestyle and psychological assessments were also made which were shared with behavioral coaches, who helped the volunteers develop and implement personalized action plans to reduce risk factors.

Multiomic data was also gathered—their genomes were sequenced, their gut bacteria sampled, as were their metabolites and proteins. This provided a total of six types of data which we would be able to mine for novel insights: clinical, lifestyle, genomics, proteomics, metabolomics and gut microbiomics.

The data was then used to tailor lifestyle intervention plans for participants. These included a range of actionable possibilities that would ameliorate or potentially reverse any risk factors for disease.

More than 14,000 statistically significant correlations between the six data types were found. Many of these correlations led to greater personalization of recommendations, such as the ability to use genetics to better optimize dietary tips. And several generated novel discoveries that could be subsequently tested in clinical trials. For example, it was found that a certain liver enzyme (gamma-glutamyl transferase, or GGT) was associated with multiple risk factors for cardiometabolic syndrome, a group of metabolic dysfunctions that raise the risk of coronary heart disease, stroke, and diabetes. We also found that higher gut microbiome diversity was associated with lower inflammatory proteins.

The hundreds or thousands of single mutations that took place during the period of this study revealed some interesting statistical correlations. For example, high risk for inflammatory bowel disease was associated with lower levels of cystine, an amino acid metabolite in the blood, and a high risk for bladder cancer was associated with higher levels of a metabolite of caffeine. These findings are useful biomarkers.

Future studies could be designed to examine the role of these biomarkers in development of disease in people who are at risk, potentially leading to future treatments or preventive strategies. More importantly, it was seen that behavioral coaching was effective in driving significant clinical improvements across various integrated biomarkers. Study participants were highly enthusiastic about this approach."

HOW TO SLOW DOWN OR REVERSE AGING

In the first chapter of this book I referred to a Danish study which established that only about 20% of how long the average person lives is dictated by our genes, whereas the other 80% is dictated by our lifestyle. Lifestyle will be discussed later in this book. For now let us now focus on the 20%.

I draw your attention to a recent article in Time Magazine by Alice Park regarding 13 years of groundbreaking breaking research into cells by Dr David Sinclair and his team. Dr Sinclair is a professor of genetics and co-director of the Paul F. Glenn Center for Biology of Aging Research at Harvard Medical School. I am grateful to Christopher K Wallace for providing the link to this article.

"Until recently, scientists had theorized that aging skin was caused by mutations in the DNA of skin. But that theory wasn't supported by the fact that older people's cells often were not riddled with mutations, and that animals or people harboring a higher burden of mutated cells don't seem to age prematurely.

Sinclair therefore focused on another part of the genome, called the epigenome. Since all cells have the same DNA blueprint, the epigenome is what makes skin cells turn into skin cells and brain cells into brain cells. It does this by providing different instructions to different cells for which genes to turn on, and which to keep silent.

Epigenetics is similar to the instructions dressmakers rely on from patterns to create shirts, pants, or jackets. The starting fabric is the same, but the pattern determines what shape and function the final article of clothing takes. With cells, the epigenetic instructions lead to cells with different physical structures and functions in a process called differentiation.

In a study published in the Cell Journal, Sinclair and his team report that not only can they age mice on an accelerated timeline, but they can also reverse the effects of that aging and restore some of the biological signs of youthfulness to the animals, in this case mice. Isn't that mind-blowing?

That reversibility makes a strong case for the fact that the main drivers of aging aren't mutations to the DNA, but miscues in the epigenetic instructions that somehow go awry. Sinclair has long proposed that aging is the result of losing critical instructions that cells need in order to continue functioning, in what he calls the Information Theory of Aging. 'Underlying aging is information that is lost in cells, not just the accumulation of damage," he says. "That's a paradigm shift in how to think about aging.

In the mice, he and his team developed a way to reboot cells to restart the backup copy of epigenetic instructions, essentially erasing the corrupted signals that put the cells on the path toward aging. They mimicked the effects of aging on the epigenome by introducing breaks in the DNA of young mice. (Outside of the lab, epigenetic changes can be driven by a number of things, including smoking, exposure to pollution and chemicals.) Once "aged" in this way, within a matter of weeks Sinclair saw that the mice began to show signs of older age—including gray fur, lower body weight despite unaltered diet, reduced activity, and increased frailty.

The rebooting came in the form of a gene therapy involving three genes that instruct cells to reprogram themselves—in the case of the mice, the instructions guided the cells to restart the epigenetic changes that defined their identity as, for example, kidney and skin cells, two cell types that are prone to the effects of aging. These genes came from the suite of so-called Yamanaka stem cells factors—a set of four genes that Nobel scientist Shinya Yamanaka in 2006 discovered can turn back the clock on adult cells to their embryonic, stem cell state so they can start their development, or differentiation process, all over again. Sinclair didn't want to completely erase the cells' epigenetic history, just reboot it enough to reset the epigenetic instructions. Using three of the four factors turned back the clock about 57%, enough to make the mice youthful again.

Rejuvenating cells in mice is one thing, but will the process work in humans? That's Sinclair's next step, and his team is already testing the system in non-human primates. The researchers are attaching a biological switch that would allow them to turn the clock on and off by tying the activation of the reprogramming genes to an antibiotic, doxycycline. Giving the animals doxycycline would start reversing the clock, and stopping the drug would halt the process. Sinclair is currently lab-testing the system with human neurons, skin, and fibroblast cells, which contribute to connective tissue."

In 2020, Sinclair reported that in mice, the process restored vision in older animals; the current results show that the system can apply to not just one tissue or organ, but the entire animal. He anticipates eye diseases will be the first condition used to test this aging reversal in people, since the gene therapy can be injected directly into the eye area.

"We had been thinking of the processes behind aging, and diseases related to aging, as irreversible," says Sinclair. "In the case of the eye, there is the misconception that you need to regrow new nerves. But in some cases the existing cells are just not functioning, so if you reboot them, they are fine. It's a new way to think about medicine."

That could mean that a host of diseases—including chronic conditions such as heart disease and even neurodegenerative disorders like Alzheimers could be treated in large part by reversing the aging process that leads to them. Even before that happens, the process could be an important new tool for researchers studying these diseases. In most cases, scientists rely on young animals or tissues to model diseases of aging, which doesn't always faithfully reproduce the condition of aging. The new system "makes the mice very old rapidly, so we can, for example, make human brain tissue the equivalent of what you would find in a 70 year old and use those in the mouse model to study Alzheimer's disease that way," Sinclair says.

This study is just the first step in redefining what it means to age, and Sinclair is the first to acknowledge that it raises more questions than answers. "We don't understand how rejuvenation really works, but we know it works," he says. "We can use it to rejuvenate parts of the body and hopefully make medicines that will be revolutionary. **Now, when I see an older person, I don't look at them as old, I just look at them as someone whose system needs to be rebooted**. It's no longer a question of if rejuvenation is possible, but a question of when."

In a previous chapter we looked at how loss of telomeric DNA can occur. Now let us look at how we can slow down this loss and deterioration. Most of these solutions will be very obvious.

If you are a smoker, cease smoking or reduce it as much as possible.

If you are obese, find ways to reduce weight - Excess weight can cause telomere shortening due to oxidative stress

If your work environment is toxic - Change your work environment. If this is not possible, seek ways through which you can detoxify.

If the type of work you do is harmful - Do your best to find a less harmful type of work. I remember quitting a job once when I found I was breathing fumes from hydrochloric acid.

If you are under constant stress - Find a way to reduce stress.

If you have a high intake of polyunsaturated fatty acids - reduce intake of these, especially linoleic acid, and increase the intake of fiber.

If your intake of protein is excessive - reduce the amount of protein intake, especially red meat. High intake of red meat leads to acidosis in the body. Acidosis has been associated with many disease states. Use plant based proteins and more carbohydrates.

STEM CELL THERAPY

While I was on a well earned vacation recently I still kept looking for useful material to include in this book. I came across something that I had touched on years ago and then faded into the background - Stem Cell Therapy.

Having asked can stem cell therapy help with anti-aging. This is the response that was readily available -

"With our current knowledge of stem cells, it is technically feasible to delay aging and improve both health and lifespan. Stem cells can play a crucial role in delaying the aging process. Stem cells, in combination with anti-aging genes, can create a sophisticated shield, which can prevent the effects of aging.

"Stem cells play a crucial role in delaying the aging process. Stem cells make a complex and protective shield, which stand against the eroding effects of aging. The shield of stem cells is a primary target for absorbing the shock of aging. If this shield neutralizes the shocks, it could lead to a youthful state. Studies suggest that stem cell interventions that increase rejuvenation and keep in balance the expression of anti-aging genes could delay aging and result in prolonged lifespan."

The benefits of a stem cell transplant for aging -

- A feeling of vitality and rejuvenation
- Improved capacity for physical activities
- Thickening and improved quality of hair
- Increased libido

- A decrease in pain
- Increased strength, balance & overall mobility
- Enhanced immunity
- Overall improvement in the quality of life
- Immune system regulation
- Decreased inflammatory markers

FOR THE LADIES

This is an article published by Ella White in March 17, 2021

"Aging is a natural process that we all go through, which affects the appearance of our skin. Many cosmetic companies market products targeted at reducing the signs of aging: in fact, in 2018 the worldwide anti-aging product market size was valued at over $38 billion and it is predicted to increase to over $60 billion by 2026. So, what are the ingredients in these widely sought-after products, and do they work?

The skin is made up of three layers. The outermost layer is called the epidermis, next is the dermis, and the bottom layer is called the subcutaneous tissue or the hypodermis. The outermost layer of the epidermis is called the stratum corneum and it is a major barrier to the penetration of many compounds into the skin. The primary target of anti-aging skin care is the epidermis-dermis junction and the dermis tissues. How deep a skin care ingredient can penetrate into the skin depends on its molecular weight and its polarity. Non-polar, low molecular weight ingredients can penetrate further.

So now that you know about the structure of skin, here's some information about the skin aging process, which is categorized as intrinsic and extrinsic aging. Intrinsic aging occurs when cell renewal takes place more slowly and there are changes in the synthesis of hormones that affect the appearance of the skin. Extrinsic aging, on the other hand, occurs as a result of lifestyle and environmental factors. It is estimated that UV radiation contributes up to 80% of extrinsic aging and other external factors include smoking, poor diet and excess alcohol intake, as well as some diseases such as diabetes.

Exposure to environmental factors can increase premature skin aging through the formation of free radicals, which have been shown to increase activity of enzymes called matrix metalloproteases (MMPs) that can degrade collagen and elastin. Decreased amounts of collagen in skin, due to an increase in its breakdown and reduced synthesis of new collagen, is a key feature of skin aging

As collagen is a necessary component of youthful skin some anti-aging skin care treatments offer formulae containing collagen. However, collagen is a triple-helix protein that is too large to be applied topically and will not penetrate the surface of the skin. Alternatively, drinks containing collagen have been marketed as anti-aging treatments but as collagen is a protein it will be digested in the stomach and broken down into amino acids. It is possible that some of these amino acids may be used to make collagen as it is such an abundant protein, but that is not necessarily the case.

A much better approach is to use products containing antioxidants which prevent free radicals causing breakdown of collagen and ingredients which stimulate collagen production. Some of these ingredients include:

- **Vitamin C** (ascorbic acid). Vitamin C is a potent antioxidant, and it has been proven to have a skin anti-aging effect by increasing collagen production and inducing inhibitors of MMPs and collagenases, which break down collagen.
- **Niacinamide** (vitamin B-3). Niacinamide is a potent antioxidant, which reduces trans-epidermal water loss and it may also improve skin elasticity.
- **Coenzyme Q10**. CoQ10 is an antioxidant, which has been shown to improve mitochondrial function in human skin samples and may therefore prevent the appearance of aging that starts at the cellular level.
- **Polyphenols.** These are naturally found in fruits, vegetables and nuts and have powerful antioxidant and photoprotective effects, reducing signs of skin aging.

- **Alpha and Beta Hydroxy acids.** (AHAs and BHAs). These weak acids chemically exfoliate the skin as well as reducing fine lines and wrinkles, and they have also been shown to induce collagen synthesis.
- **Peptides**. Some peptides, such as palmitoyl pentapeptide-3, have been shown to stimulate collagen production, and in doing so they improve skin texture and reduce wrinkles.
- **Retinoids** (Vitamin A compounds, such as retinol and retinoic acid). Vitamin A and its derivatives are some of the most effective substances to slow down the aging process. Retinoids reduce signs of aging by reducing trans-epidermal water loss and increasing the protective function of the epidermis, as well as increasing collagen in the skin by inhibiting MMP activity and reducing collagen degradation"

Over the counter (OTC) cosmetics may contain some retinoids and offer some anti aging benefits but not in strong enough concentration to be pharmacologically active. Furthermore cosmetics are not required to undergo rigid clinical trials and testing such as pharmaceutical medicines must undergo. Rigid clinical trials and testing are an expensive process and if it was carried out for cosmetics then they could be classified as medicines.

Vitamin A however, is the first vitamin approved by the American Food and Drug Administration (FDA) as an anti-wrinkle agent: Tazarotene, for example, is a vitamin A prescription medication that can be applied topically to improve sun-damaged skin and decrease signs of wrinkles.

Prescription retinoids are more potent than OTC products and although there may be strong evidence that retinoids reduce signs of aging, there is less evidence that OTC retinoids will make a difference.

COMPOUNDS THAT CONTRIBUTE TO LONGEVITY

I use Google for research when writing a book. For this book I was searching for available anti-aging treatments. At first I was disappointed because all I could find was skin treatments for ladies - botox, fillers, dermabrasion etc. But by tweaking my search keywords I found a product by Perpetual Life called AEON Longevity Complex.

I do not believe there is a "Magic Pill" that will keep you young. There may be some benefits in taking a supplement but many other factors such as health status, nutrition, exercise and possible interaction with medications should be considered before spending your hard earned cash. Nevertheless most of the reviews on this particular supplement have been positive.

AEON Longevity Complex contains the following compounds.

- Nicotinamide Mononucleotide
- Quercetin

- Trans-resveratrol
- L-Theanine
- Fisetin
- Astragalus
- Tetrahydrocurcumin
- Collagen
- CoQ10
- Crocin
- Epigallocatechin Gallate

Having done studies in Botanical Medicine and attended many seminars, I read the notes provided for each of the above compounds with intention to evaluate what research had been done to validate the use of the compounds in this product.

Validation of the compound's effectiveness has come from both animal and human studies. This is what I surmise about the compounds -

Nicotinamide Mononucleotide - *(NAD+)* Short term studies have shown some benefits but more numbers and longer term studies are needed.

Quercetin - Good if dosages are not too high otherwise may be potential risk for kidney damage

Trans-resveratrol - Resveratrol has been touted as an potent antioxidant for a long time

L-Theanine - A component of Green Tea has many advocates

Fisetin - Is found in a number of fruits and vegetables and could be effective against numerous diseases

Astragalus - Is well known in Chinese Medicine with centuries of use

Tetrahydrocurcumin - This is obtained from Turmeric which is used extensively in Indian cuisine, a good antioxidant

Collagen - Involved mainly in skin repair to reduce wrinkles and possibly prevent more wrinkling

CoQ10 - CoQ10 has shown therapeutic benefits in aging-related disorders, particularly in cardiovascular and metabolic diseases.

Crocin - From Saffron, a very pricey spice has shown many health benefits including anticancer, anti-inflammatory, anti-anxiety, and antidiabetic effects

Epigallocatechin Gallate - From tea leaves, including green tea. I wouldn't dare criticize tea

WHAT I LEARNED OVER THE YEARS

Being now into the latter half of my seventies I believe that what I've learned over the years will benefit younger readers.

What I noticed as I was heading towards my seventies was the attitudes of slightly older relatives around me who upon being asked "how are you?" would respond "like the oldies." And I looked around and I wondered how some "oldies" looked older than others of the same age. Do some Imitate or "model" aging from seeing older people? Do they believe that they must walk like old people? hunch like old people?, drag their feet like old people and so on? I began thinking that maybe people age because they let go of youthful activity or they believe they have to behave like adults and conform to social "norms." In other words they have to look like and become oldies?

I remember having read about a social experiment carried out in the US in the nineteen nineties. Several octogenarians were invited to attend a weekend event held at a resort. They were to come dressed as they had dressed in the nineteen fifties. The resort was decorated in fifties style and there were vintage cars parked in the driveway for added effect. In the resort they played fifties music and danced like in the fifties.

Immediately following the event, the octogenarians reported they felt younger, more energetic, felt hardly any of the aches and pains they had been feeling and said they had regained some of their youthful vitality.

Followed up twelve months after they had returned home many of them had gone back to being alone at home, not engaging in much activity and feeling their "age" and "aches and pains" again. What does this tell you?

To me this indicates that the environment has a lot to do with the process of aging, and that activity and stimulation can be essential factors that slow down the aging process and maintain youthfulness.

So what of this have I applied to my life?

Yes, I went through a few periods of depression, loss of interest and lack of activity in the nineteen seventies and eighties. Once I got past this I felt invigorated and it was like I wanted to do everything at once! That was until I was struck down with cancer, surgery and chemotherapy that led to life-threatening effects.

Nevertheless I recovered and got back into the workforce and into my hypnotherapy practice. A good friend, who was a radiographer and psychologist, encouraged me to take up kayaking again which I had stopped during my recovery. I took up bass guitar again and joined a Rock and Blues Jam group.

At first it took a lot of effort to get to the practice sessions but once we did a couple gigs, one of which I organized as a fundraiser for OXFAM, I was all revved up and keen to form my own band. The band "COOL HEAT" is still active at the time of writing, we aim to rehearse every week and look forward to doing more gigs.

My nutrition has also improved. I had been skimping on meals and drinking more cheap red wine than I should have. Once I acquired better eating habits and stopped the wine I felt stronger, had greater vitality and strength. A small amount of quality wine can be good for health, but not in my case because of damage to my body from cancer, surgery and chemotherapy. I have finally recovered from all that!

If you recall from.chapter 2 "The world's longest-lived people do not pump iron, run marathons, or join gyms." They benefit from natural activity.

As a writer, I am sitting a lot of the time and I don't have too much activity so I compensate for this with daily walks, brief repetitions with two 5 Kg (11 lbs) dumbbells and the occasional kayaking when weather and tides are favorable.

I also meditate twice daily, facilitate a meditation session once a week and volunteer at a mental health recreational center. Of late I have applied to be a voluntary health educator for seniors in the local community. Then there is the sporadic overseas travel which is always invigorating, even though it seems tiring at the time.

The main take-aways from this chapter is, keep active, exercise, eat healthy, laugh, have fun!

WHAT TO START DOING RIGHT NOW

From a Facebook post -

Stop Using Your Age As An Excuse...

At any age, **lift weights**.
At any age, **write books.**
At any age, **find new love.**
At any age, **start a business.**
At any age, **claim mountains.**
At any age, **create a new you.**

You're not dead until you're dead.

And what you can do is stop thinking of yourself as old. Once you stop this, it can trigger a new way of thinking, feeling and functioning. Just a small shift in perspective can make a BIG difference.

3664247 © Pavel Losevsky | Dreamstime.com

See your reality in a different way. The thought came to me this morning when I was on the bus to the local shopping mall to fill a script at the pharmacy.

I can understand how easy it would be for one to get jaded as years go by. The self-talk could go something like this - " ... Bugger! I've run out of meds again! Now I'll have to go to the mall, what an effort it's going to be, to catch the bus and ride among all those strangers, then I'll have to wait for the pharmacist to prepare the prescription … can't stand waiting … then get a bus back, blah blah blah …"

Alternatively the whole thing could be perceived as a healthy outing - a walk to the bus station, enjoying the diversity of different passengers on the bus, interacting with the staff at the pharmacy. All these experiences should not be trivialized or complained about. It's your life, and once you're dead, you'll never have the same experiences again. So GET WITH IT!

You have read about Blue Zones and what contributes to healthy aging and vitality. It is obvious that you would need to be in those parts of the world and live the same lifestyle to experience the same level of health and vitality. But a change of outlook and a different mindset will help greatly.

And there are changes you can make even at this stage of your life in order to restore strength and vitality. For example yesterday I paddled my friend's kayak at Botany Bay. It was a very hot day, there was a swell rolling in towards shore and the water was chopped up further because of speedboats and water skis. This made the experience more exciting as well as providing healthy sunshine, fresh sea air and exercise.

Research has shown that engaging in that kind of activity or even a twenty minute walk can ease your mind into releasing anxieties and the cares of day to day living. This "break" can only be beneficial toward restoration of health and vitality. The body is doing what it is designed to do, engaging in physical activity.

An article published by Joanna Colek back in 2018 explains how you can calm your anxious mind through rhythmic movement. As we already know, anxiety and stress contribute to aging. Colek gives examples of rhythmic activity, including walking. This is the list from her article, according to what works for her. I believe walking is very important. You will understand why as you read on. Some of the other activities could appeal to you as well -

1. Walking
Walking is one of the easiest anxiety-reducing movement-based techniques. It can invoke mindfulness, clear your head, and release stress from the body. And if done in nature, you will feel more awake and alert and, at the same time, open, relaxed, and spacious.

2. Hatha yoga
The most rewarding for me personally, Hatha yoga is a gentle practice of body-mind integration. Yoga combines awareness of breathing with asana practice, enabling you to achieve the state of mindfulness and wholeness. It's easy and accessible to everyone—you don't have to join a studio, simply search YouTube for inspiration and lesson videos.

3. Gardening

Nothing connects me more to my surroundings than gardening. Great for anxiety and taming the monkey mind, gardening is a perfect activity to help you become mindful and engage with the world around you with all your senses. The calm of gardening can bring about the state of flow, as you become fully absorbed in the activity. Gardening is grounding; my garden is my personal Zen.

4. Swimming

Swimming is a gentle exercise that allows you to focus on deep breathing and the rhythm of your stroke, both lulling you into a state of deep relaxation. It comes with minimal distractions and is a great tension reliever. All you need is a body of water.

5. Dancing

Focused on expression on a bodily level, dancing allows you to tap into your body's own healing resources. It's therapeutic. You connect with your body in elemental ways and allow it to express feelings often hard to convey in words—something especially beneficial for trauma victims and people suffering from anxiety or depression.

By being mindful while dancing, you also learn about yourself and your body and embrace your creativity and the comforting flow of pleasant physical sensations, fully re-engaging with the present moment. And that's healing.

To this list I personally add Vedic Meditation, which I do twice daily. See thomknoles.com for more information on this.

Our distant ancestors would not have been sitting at a computer or lounging in front of a TV eating pizza or snacking on chips. Their day would have consisted of hunting for game or looking for edible fruits and roots. This would have required a lot of walking.

Come the evening there would have been enough time to cook and eat with the tribe thus providing a sense of community and belonging. When it got dark, all retired to the cave or hut for a good night's sleep to wake up fresh the following morning.

During the process of our evolution our ancestors started to cultivate crops and storing grain. Hunting and gathering need not have been as essential as it had been. Consequently a more sedentary lifestyle became possible. This had advantages and disadvantages. The advantage being that people had time to develop crafts and engage in other sedentary activities. The disadvantage was that the lack of physical activity partly led to obesity and consequent ill effects from it.

Nevertheless communities of those days were still small enough to provide for most individuals a sense of belonging. Most likely they knew each other, even on a passing by basis. You can imagine, for example, waving to the blacksmith as you walked past his workshop, or exchanging pleasantries with the baker when you bought your bread. This was a good thing.

Going forward to the industrial revolution people moved from small farming communities and cottage industries to the cities. The sense of belonging and community was lost. From cottage industry and small family concerns many found it necessary to work in mills and factories where the atmosphere was generally non-personal.

Looking back at the Blue Zones research, it is seen that a sense of belonging, family and community was one of the factors that contributed to that longevity.

At the risk of sounding repetitive here are 5 tips to help you stay youthful and healthy as you age.

1. Stay positive. One of the best-known ways to keep feeling young is having a positive mental outlook....
2. Stay active. Regular exercise lowers the risk of heart disease, diabetes, arthritis, obesity and dementia....
3. Stay connected....
4. Eat the right foods....
5. Try something new…

You can have fun at any age

WHAT THE FUTURE HOLDS

Back In 2008, Dan Buettner and the Blue Zones team used established methodologies to try to determine why people had such remarkable longevity in the Blue Zone areas. The intent, Buettner explained, was to identify lessons or principles that could be applied to build healthier communities and to help people live longer and better lives.

The team then finalized the blueprint for "Life Radius," a blueprint that could be applied to American cities. This was exciting. Local government town planners and other influential personnel were approached with suggested changes they could make to city environments to make it more healthy for people. In some cities ``Green Zones' ' were created by turning areas into pedestrian only zones. Walking paths were established, trees and shrubs were planted. Restaurant owners were encouraged to offer more green entrees and deli owners started offering healthier options.

Coming up to scratch with the people who live in the Blue Zones may not be a possibility. But you can start afresh from where you are in life. Lifestyle is always something that can be improved. The reduction of smoking, alcohol consumption, junk food eating are certainly within your reach and within your control and so too overeating.

I tried to find out what was currently happening with this blueprint and was led to https://www.sharecare.com/blue-zones-project . There I found this Blue Zones Project® was helping transform communities across North America into areas where the healthy choice is easy and people live longer with a higher quality of life.

Following through I discovered another website - sharecare.com. This website focuses on improvement and maintenance of health and wellbeing. It helps nearly 10 million employees, plan members and patients better understand their health, optimize their benefits, address critical care gaps, and improve health outcomes while helping to lower the cost of care.

This quote is from sharecare.com - "Everyone lives better, longer. That's the vision. We're making strides every day by bringing together the many different elements of health for you, your family, and your community. It's not easy connecting doctors, health plans, employers, useful tools, quality information, and more to deliver what you need when you need it. But that's what makes Sharecare special. We're putting the power of living your healthiest life in your hands."

The environment within which you live can either be improved or you can move to a more healthy environment. You can get out of toxic relationships or a toxic work environment. You can attend local government meetings, rally others to your cause, and lobby for changes in your district.

And there are so many developments and discoveries in medicine. Only recently did I read about a cure for a childhood brain cancer that has proved fatal up till now. Lymphocytes are extracted from a patient's blood, genetically modified then returned to the patient's bloodstream where they help to fight the cancer cells.

Just yesterday the headline from our local newspaper announced a young child's life in our neighborhood was saved by this treatment. This type of biotechnology will undoubtedly lead to development of other medical breakthroughs, including antiaging.

NEUROGENESIS

A study done in 2017 demonstrated that there is a relationship between exercise and creation of new neurons. Creation of new neurons can stave off Alzheimer's disease by 20 years.

Creation of new neurons and neural pathways also occurs when you learn new skills or part-take in mentally challenging tasks.

CANNABIS

Studies done with mice have demonstrated that dosing older mice with THC resulted in gene activity and the molecular profile in the brain tissue like that of much younger animals. Specifically, neurons in the hippocampus grew more synaptic spines— points of contact necessary for communication between neurons.

Neurobiology professor Andreas Zimmer, University of Bonn, suggests THC may be involved in the regulation of the aging process). The team is now planning tests to see if the same holds true in human subjects.

In a 2014 study, researchers at the University of South Florida and Thomas Jefferson University found that low-dose THC directly impedes the build-up of beta amyloid plaque in the brain, which is associated with the development of Alzheimer's, and unlike so many pharmaceutical drugs, it produces no toxicity. THC was also found to enhance mitochondrial function in the brain. Lead author and neuroscientist Chuanhai Cao, Ph.D., wrote:

"THC is known to be a potent antioxidant with neuroprotective properties, but this is the first report that the compound directly affects Alzheimer's pathology by decreasing amyloid beta levels, inhibiting its aggregation and enhancing mitochondrial function."

Cannabis is also known to reduce some of the non-memory-related symptoms typically experienced by Alzheimer's sufferers, including anxiety, irritability and rage, so cannabis may well have multiple benefits for those with dementia and Alzheimer's.

CANNABIS FOR CHRONIC PAIN

The following extract is the conclusion reached in an article published in the Australian Journal of of General Practice Volume 50, Issue 10, October 2021 -

"Medicinal cannabis is worthy of consideration in the management of chronic pain, and it is important that doctors are aware of the positives and negatives related to its use. The more commonly prescribed oral products (oils, sprays and capsules) are attractive since they can be delivered in a more controlled and socially acceptable manner than inhaled products, although they have a slower onset.

While CBD products are attractive given better safety when driving or performing other safety-sensitive tasks, current supportive evidence for their efficacy is limited.

Harm minimisation should always be front of mind in prescribing decisions, particularly with patients who are driving regularly or using heavy machinery.

It must be recognised that the long-term effects of medicinal cannabis, potential drug–drug interactions and efficacy across different pain types remain only partly understood. The guiding principle of start low, go slow is crucial, with the aim to obtain clinical benefits at the lowest possible dose and to minimize risks and side effects.

A recent and authoritative systematic review, commissioned by the International Association for the Study of Pain, concluded that the current evidence 'neither supports nor refutes claims of efficacy and safety for cannabinoids, cannabis, or cannabis-based medicines in the management of pain' and that there is 'the pressing need for studies to fill the research gap,' a conclusion supported by another recent systematic review.

The Faculty of Pain Medicine of the Australian and New Zealand College of Anaesthetists concluded that until higher quality evidence is available, currently available cannabinoid products should only be prescribed as part of a registered clinical trial.

Despite the fact that current supportive evidence is of low overall quality, there are tens of thousands of patients with chronic pain being prescribed medicinal cannabis products in Australia, and hundreds of thousands using illicit cannabis products to self-medicate chronic pain. Many have legitimate lived experience of lasting pain reduction with cannabis that is not easily disregarded.

There is clearly a disconnection between the pronouncements of specialist medical colleges and current prescribing and community use of cannabinoids in Australia. It is hoped that the results of the next generation of clinical trials of cannabinoid products and pain will help to resolve this tension."

The following words were spoken to me by a male of seventy years who has suffered pain from a bunion for a number of years. *"This cannabis oil works much better than the Panadeine Forte* (Paracetamol and Codeine) *that I've been taking all these years."*

OTHER DRUGS

Scientists are great at making mice live longer and experimental studies with mice can eventually lead up to useful applications that can then be tested on humans.

For example Rapamycin, widely prescribed to prevent organ rejection after a transplant, increases the life expectancy of middle-age mice by as much as 60 percent. Drugs called senolytics help geriatric mice stay sprightly long after their peers have died. The diabetes drugs metformin and acarbose, extreme calorie restriction, and, by one biotech investor's count, about 90 other interventions keep mice skittering around lab cages well past their usual expiration date. The newest scheme is to hack the aging process itself by reprogramming old cells to a younger state.

Gregory Fahy's experiment published in 2019 provided the tantalizing suggestion that a medical intervention might lower a person's biological age. Fahy and other scientists are now participants in the larger trial Fahy is conducting.

At the time of writing Fahy described his mother Dorothy, who outlived her husband, her two younger sisters, and a late-life boyfriend. "Her short gray bob is always salon perfect. She is thin and walks slowly, with a cane, but she stands straight. On most weekdays she goes to her neighborhood senior center, where she takes exercise classes, dances, and eats lunch with friends. She never forgets a birthday or a bill due."

Fahy, whose primary interest was in the thymus, believed that immunological aging could be reversed by treating the thymus, a small gland in the chest that stimulates the development of disease-fighting T cells. On and off for eight years he injected himself with recombinant human growth hormone (HGH), a drug used for decades to treat children with short stature.

He theorized that it could rejuvenate the thymus and the body's waning defenses against disease. However HGH is also associated with an elevated risk of some cancers. Fahy said "I took matters into my own hands and started regenerating my own thymus based on what I could glean from the rat study." But because the drug can raise the risk of type 2 diabetes, he added two pills: metformin and dehydroepiandrosterone, or DHEA, a hormone that improves blood-sugar regulation.

Both are also thought to mitigate the effects of aging, and they're commonly used for that purpose. Metformin, which is taken for diabetes by 150 million people worldwide, may reduce the incidence of neurodegenerative diseases and cancer.

US researchers are planning a study to see if it prevents or delays major age-related illnesses. Some longevity scientists aren't waiting: They pop metformin daily.

Walt Crompton, a retired biomedical engineer in Silicon Valley joined Fahy with this regimen. He said he immediately felt the effects of this regimen. "It seemed like I could leap tall buildings in a single bound." He shed unwanted pounds without dieting. Another participant, Hank Pellissier, 70, said his hair, previously white, began growing brown.

Tests showed that T cell production increased with the treatment, thymus fat disappeared, and kidney and prostate health improved. Most striking, the men lost an average of two and a half years of biological age, as measured by what's known as an epigenetic clock. It uses blood to measure chemical changes to DNA that alter gene expression and mark the passage of time.

A study done in 2022 published in the Journal of Theranostics concluded that Metformin has significant effects in anti-aging and in attenuating aging-related diseases and displays promising perspective in aging-related clinical applications.

However, distinct molecular mechanisms through which metformin attenuates aging and different aging-related diseases are still poorly understood and remain to be investigated in great detail.

Better understanding of these mechanisms will greatly facilitate the development of novel and efficient strategies for the prevention and treatment of aging and aging-related diseases by metformin.

EXERCISE

A recent study showed that imitating Mr T Bags walk in the "Ministry of Silly Walks" (John Cleese) provides about seven times more exercise than regular walking. So if you substitute this walk during your normal walk time you will benefit from the exponentially increased exercise. See https://www.youtube.com/watch?v=eCLp7zodUiI

Laughter has also been shown to be beneficial in the slowing down of the aging process. You have probably experienced this to a certain extent in your own life; recall how good you have felt after a good laugh.

Motivation to exercise can differ from person to person. The reason once given for this was character or personality trait. Scientists were not content with this vague explanation and went on to seek other causes.

Motivation, they found, was correlated with the level of dopamine. Furthermore it was found that certain kinds of gut bacteria produced dopamine. Therefore the motivation to exercise could be improved by correcting the balance of dopamine producing bacteria in the gut.

A news release from the University of Pennsylvania Trustees News, December 14, 2022 said. "Researchers from the university and other researchers were able to determine that two specific gut bacteria Eubacterium rectale and Coprocopous eutactus increased exercise capacity in mice. Study co-author, J. Nicholas Betley, PhD, an associate professor of Biology at the University of Pennsylvania's School of Arts and Sciences, said "This line of research could develop into a whole new branch of exercise physiology."

Apart from possibly offering cheap, safe, diet-based ways of getting ordinary people running and optimizing elite athletes' performance, he added, the exploration of this pathway might also yield easier methods for modifying motivation and mood in settings such as addiction and depression.

THE BENEFITS OF COPROCOCCUS

Coprococcus may play an important role in host health by its production of vitamins B and SCFAs, whereas another species, Lachnoclostridium, might have an opposing effect by influencing negatively the circulating levels of acetate and being involved in the biosynthesis of detrimental lipid compounds.

JOE DISPENSA

Joe Dispenza says epigenetics research has shown that you can change your body by thought alone. The process would be arduous, but the belief is that it can be done, and I imagine that determination, mindset and attitude would play major roles.

NUTRITION

Permeability of the epithelial intestinal barrier is known to increase with age. Otherwise known as "Leaky Gut Syndrome" this can lead to more inflammation in the body.

Today, many foods are known to be potent Nrf2 activators The Mrf2 biological pathway activated by this activator stimulates cells to produce antioxidants. Some of these antioxidant-packed foods are:

- Dark chocolate or cacao nibs
- Vegetables – cruciferous vegetables in particular like cauliflower, bok choy, and broccoli microgreens
- Herbs and spices – especially cloves, ginger, cinnamon, turmeric, yellow mustard, and oregano
- Legumes
- Red wine – must be red because the grape skin contains most of the antioxidants
- Tea, especially white and green teas

FASTING

The benefits of intermittent fasting have been shown many times over. If in doubt about fasting check with your doctor. Not snacking in between meals is a good thing too. And it's always better to not fill the stomach too much. Leave just a tiny bit of hunger so that you look forward to and enjoy the next meal better.

STEM CELL THERAPY AND THE KLOTHO GENE

As already mentioned in a previous chapter Stem cells can play a crucial role in delaying the aging process. Stem cells, in combination with anti-aging genes, can create a sophisticated shield, which can prevent the effects of aging.

I have taken extracts from an article by Authors Mujid Ullah and Zhongiie Sun of the Department of Physiology, BMSB, College of Medicine, University of Oklahoma Health Sciences Center. The article is available under the creative commons act (http://creativecommons.org/licenses/by/4.0/)

"In the future aging could probably be delayed for some time using the latest scientific discoveries. These discoveries would introduce the latest technologies to control and reprogram the genes and stem cells involved in aging. Restoration of youthful gene expression would enable cells to grow younger. Restoring the youthful gene expression may help turn back the clock on aging and potentially extend the healthy lifespan. Responsible factors could be of a genetic, nongenetic, and environmental origin.

On the genetic side, this could involve modulating the expression of Klotho, AMPK, cyclin A2, FGF21, FOXN1, GDF11, Oct4, PGC-1, TGF-β1, apolipoprotein A-1, and I am not dead yet (INDY), the genes responsible for life extension.

On the environmental side, foods, nutrients, vitamins, and medications make us healthier, probably because they induce the expression of health-promoting genes and reduce the expression of disease-promoting genes. Conversely, the consumption of toxic substances including chemicals, smoke, drugs, and alcohol do the reverse.

Regenerative therapies concentrate their focus on stem cells and other life-extending factors and seek attention to reverse aging. Nevertheless, the potential of stem cells to be used as therapeutic cargo has had a profound effect on the vision of the future of regenerative medicine. Aged tissues have a limited stem cell reservoir, decreased population, and low renewal efficiency. All of these are the contributing factors for cellular senescence, apoptosis, autophagy, and oxidative stress, which finally accumulate and lead to aging.

Anti-aging therapies are a new emerging era of science that seem to benefit society using the power of stem cells, cytokines, and growth, regenerative, and life-extending factors. Future scientific discoveries will unravel these puzzles of aging biology. Probably, such life-extending factors mobilize the endogenous stem cells or renew or increase their number and functions.

Regenerative therapies and exogenous stem cell transplantation into damaged tissues will also improve the wear and tear of aging.

Aging is not just due to local wear and tear. It is a process (a cumulative process of damage), and the process may be controlled in a significant way. Stem cells are an excellent candidate for regenerative medicine; however, it is important to understand that these miraculous cells may indeed be the future of medicine for mainstream cellular therapies of aging. Aging science is in its infancy, but it is clearly leading to the time when scientists will develop genetic engineering and stem cell therapies that will enable us to reverse aging and help us to grow younger and healthier."

Abbreviations used in this article -

AMPK - Adenosine monophosphate-activated protein kinase

FGF2 - Fibroblast growth factor 2

FOX11 - Forkhead box N1

GDF1 - Growth differentiation factor 1

IGF1 - Insulin-like growth factor 1

INDY - I am not dead yet

KL - Klotho

MSC - Mesenchymal stromal cells

Oct-4 - Octamer-binding transcription factor 4

PGC1 - Proliferator-activated receptor-gamma coactivator 1

ROS - Reactive oxygen species

SUM01 - Small ubiquitin-like modifier 1

TGF-β - Transforming growth factor beta

Wnt - Wingless-type MMTV integration site family member

The above article dates back to January 2018. A later article in the Genetic Engineering and Biotechnology News Dated January 24, 2023 reported how -

"In vitro and in vivo studies have shown how an anti-aging gene identified in a population of centenarians can rewind the heart's biological age by ten years. The discovery, led by scientists at the University of Bristol and the MultiMedica Group in Italy, could represent a breakthrough that offers a potential target for patients with heart failure.

In their newly reported research, the team, co-led by Paolo Madeddu, MD, Professor of Experimental Cardiovascular Medicine at the Bristol Heart Institute, University of Bristol, demonstrated that the longevity-associated variant (LAV) of the BPIFB4 gene, which is particularly frequent in centenarians, can protect cells collected from patients with heart failure requiring cardiac transplantation. The team also found that a single administration of the LAV-BPIFB4 gene, halted the decay of heart function in middle-aged mice. Even more remarkably, when given to elderly mice – whose hearts exhibit the same alterations observed in elderly patients – the gene rewound the heart's biological clock age by the human equivalent of more than ten years.

Puca, who is head of the laboratory at the IRCCS MultiMedica and Professor at the University of Salerno, further pointed out, "Gene therapy with the healthy gene in mouse models of disease has already been shown to prevent the onset of atherosclerosis, vascular aging, and diabetic complications, and to rejuvenate the immune system. "We have a new confirmation and enlargement of the therapeutic potential of the gene/protein. We hope to test its effectiveness soon in clinical trials on patients with heart failure."

The team stated in their paper, "Additional efficacy/safety studies toward regulatory approval of the longevity gene/protein will determine if this new technology can introduce a change in the prevention and treatment of age-related disease, restoring health rather than amending the damage inflicted by aging."

Professor James Leiper, PhD, Associate Medical Director at the British Heart Foundation, which partly funded the research, said, "We all want to know the secrets of aging and how we might slow down age-related disease.

Our heart function declines with age but this research has extraordinarily revealed that a variant of a gene that is commonly found in long-lived people can halt and even reverse aging of the heart in mice. This is still early-stage research but could one day provide a revolutionary way to treat people with heart failure and even stop the debilitating condition from developing in the first place."

EXAMPLES OF PEOPLE WHO LIVED A YOUTHFUL LIFE

MADAM JEANNE LOUISE CALMENT

This article is from a Facebook community page "Daily Dose of Kindness." It came to me as a post suggested by Facebook. It was included here as an inspiration and not necessarily as a plan to follow.

"Meet Madame Jeanne Louise Calment, who had the longest confirmed human lifespan: 122 years, 164 days. Apparently, fate strongly approved of the way she lived her life. She was born in Arles, France, on February 21, 1875. The Eiffel Tower was built when she was 14 years old. It was at this time she met Vincent van Gogh. "He was dirty, badly dressed, and disagreeable," she recalled in an interview given in 1988.

When she was 85, she took up fencing, and still rode her bike when she reached 100. At the age of 114, she starred in a film about her life, at age 115 she had an operation on her hip, and at age 117 she gave up smoking, having started at the age of 21 in 1896. She didn't give it up for health reasons; her reason was that she didn't like having to ask someone to help her light a cigarette once she was nearly blind.

In 1965, Jeanne was 90 years old and had no heirs. She signed a deal to sell her apartment to a 47-year-old lawyer called André-François Raffray. He agreed to pay her a monthly sum of 2,500 francs on the condition he would inherit her apartment after she died. However, Raffray not only ended up paying Jeanne for 30 years, but then died before she did at the age of 77. His widow was legally obliged to continue paying Madam Calment until the end of her days.

Jeanne retained sharp mental faculties. When she was asked on her 120th birthday what kind of future she expected to have. Her reply, "A very short one."

Here are the Rules of Life from Jeanne Louise Calment:

"I'm in love with wine."
"All babies are beautiful."
"I think I will die of laughter."
"I've been forgotten by our Good Lord."
"I've got only one wrinkle, and I'm sitting on it."

"I never wear mascara; I laugh until I cry often."
"If you can't change something, don't worry about it."
"Always keep your smile. That's how I explain my long life."
"I see badly, I hear badly, and I feel bad, but everything's fine."
"I have a huge desire to live and a big appetite, especially for sweets."
"I have legs of iron, but to tell you the truth, they're starting to rust and buckle a bit."
"I took pleasure when I could. I acted clearly and morally and without regret. I'm very lucky."
"Being young is a state of mind, it doesn't depend on one's body. I'm actually still a young girl, it's just that I haven't looked so good for the past 70 years."

At the end of one interview, the journalist said, "Madame, I hope we will meet again sometime next year." To which Jeanne replied, "Why not? You're not that old; you'll still be here!"

(The image with the wings is a piece of art by L. Lichtenfells)

TAT WALE BABA

As a contrast to Madame Jeanne Calment I present to you Tat Wale Baba. Tat Wale baba was born on July 24, 1890 in Punjab, India. He seems to be around 40

years old in the photo, but is actually 82. Babaji entered Mahāsamādhi in 1974, but as he once said to a spiritual aspirant:

"That which is unborn, eternal, we can't talk about it in terms of time. In terms of time the Self can't be talked about."

Tat Wale Baba was famous in Rishikesh and all over India. He was known as the "naked saint" or "the wise man of the mountains' '. Tat Wale was a nickname meaning "one who wears jute". Baba means "father".

As an eremitic sage, he gave regular audiences to visitors for a short time but rarely left his humble Ashram. Spiritual aspirants came to get advice or simply meditate in his presence and get his blessing. Even today, many pilgrims visit his cave.

SUMMARY

Now you have read the book you will have discovered some ways that you can keep or regenerate youthful enthusiasm and vitality. If you need, go back and reread what you may have missed.

Depending on what you scored in chapter 3 there are always mobility aids and other ways to get about, unless of course you are bedridden or simply don't want to.

You can be more responsible with dietary choices and choices regarding smoking, drinking etc.

My routine is to go for a walk and a little workout on dumbbells daily. Although I am sitting down writing this book at present I try to keep more active and to not habituate to a sedentary lifestyle. And don't forget intermittent fasting.

There are plenty of activities or hobbies in which you can participate. Also make sure you keep your mind active and engaged because this will prevent or delay Alzheimer's or dementia.

You have now become aware of current research, products available and future direction of anti-aging research which could lead to procedures that will soon be available to you. Even without those, plenty of other avenues have been presented to you.

In closing I wish you the best of luck on your journey of rejuvenation.

The author,
Alfred.

GLOSSARY

Apoptosis - The death of cells which occurs as a normal and controlled part of an organism's growth or development

Autophagy - Consumption of the body's own tissue as a metabolic process occurring in starvation and certain diseases

Blue Zones - Places in the world where people live the longest and are the healthiest

Cellular senescence - The process by which cells age

Endogenous - From within the body

Epigenome - The "template" from which the genome is formed

Epigenetics - The science behind the epigenome

Exogenous - From outside the body

Genome - The entire set of DNA instructions found in a cell

Homeostasis - A state of balance among all the body systems needed for the body to survive and function correctly

Multiomics - A new approach where the datasets of different omic groups are combined during analysis

Omic groups - The branches of science known informally as omics are various disciplines in biology

Proteomics - The science about proteins

SCFA - Short Chain Fatty Acids

Telomeres - The specific Protein structures found at both ends of each chromosome

Theranostics - Refers to the pairing of diagnostic biomarkers with therapeutic agents that share a specific target in diseased cells or tissues.

Oxidative stress - A condition that may occur when there are too many unstable molecules called free radicals in the body and not enough antioxidants to get rid of them. This can lead to cell and tissue damage.

REFERENCES

The role of physical activity in healthy aging - WHO_APR_AHE_98.2 Heikkinen

https://www.who.int/news-room/questions-and-answers/item/healthy-ageing-and-functional-ability

https://liveup.org.au/get-started

https://liveup.org.au/

https://www.ncbi.nlm.nih.gov/pmc/articles/PMC6125071/

https://www.agingresearch.org/

https://www.gov.uk/government/publications/healthy-ageing/healthy-ageing-applying-all-our-health

American Journal of Lifestyle Medicine - 2016 Sep-Oct; 10(5): 318–321

https://www.ncbi.nlm.nih.gov/pmc/articles/PMC6125071/

Alice Park https://time.com/6246864/reverse-aging-scientists-discover-milestone/

https://www.scientificamerican.com/custom-media/the-new-science-of-wellness/

https://www.bluezones.com/2018/08/future-of-health-care-is-creating-environmental-change/

https://www.frontiersin.org/articles/10.3389/fpsyt.2013.00071/full

https://www.pacesconnection.com/blog/calming-your-anxious-mind-through-rhythmic-movement?nc=1#:~:text=Rhythmic%20movement%2C%20just%20like%20meditation,activities%20are%20grounding%20as%20well.

https://www.ncbi.nlm.nih.gov/pmc/articles/PMC3370421/

Aging Cell Journal of 2022; 12(6): 2722–2740

https://www.youtube.com/watch?v=e4h7okNdC1M

https://www.youtube.com/watch?v=dCokWcIcmuc

https://www.pacesconnection.com/blog/calming-your-anxious-mind-through-rhythmic-movement?nc=1

https://www.pennmedicine.org/news/news-releases/2022/december/

https://www.dvcstem.com/

https://www.ncbi.nlm.nih.gov/pmc/articles/PMC5763529/

https://www.genengnews.com/aging/anti-aging-gene-rewinds-by-a-decade-the-hearts-biological-age/

https://www.heartfoundation.org.au/

https://www.heartfoundation.org.au/getmedia/6c33122b-475c-4531-8c26-7e7a7b0eb7c1/Blueprint-For-An-Active-Australia.pdf

https://getanimated.uk.com/the-science-behind-anti-aging-skincare/

https://www1.racgp.org.au/ajgp/2021/october/medicinal-cannabis

http://creativecommons.org/licenses/by/4.0/

https://www.youtube.com/watch?v=eCLp7zodUiI

Printed in Dunstable, United Kingdom

66676252R00057